PAIR'D

A DATING GUIDE TO REAL ESTATE
PARTNERSHIPS

NIKKI MERKERSON

Dedication

To My Children,

Everything I've learned, I've learned the hard way. Every mistake, every setback, every unexpected challenge has been a lesson that shaped me. If I only knew then what I know now, the journey might have been easier—but then, I wouldn't have the wisdom to pass down to you.

This book is my way of making sure you don't have to learn everything the hard way. It's a guide to choosing the right partners, protecting what you build, and walking into every opportunity with clarity and confidence.

May you always trust your instincts, do your due diligence, and never be afraid to take bold steps toward your future. I wrote this so you can stand on my lessons, not repeat them.

With all my love and hope for your success,
Mom

CONTENTS

CONTENTS

Introduction:
When Real Estate Meets Romance

It was a Tuesday morning in my office when Kiana and Anthony walked in, high school best friends with steady jobs, good credit scores, and a shared dream of buying their first property in Brooklyn. They had known each other for fifteen years, trusted each other completely, and were convinced their friendship could weather any storm.

"We're tired of paying three thousand each in rent," Kiana explained. "We figured, why not buy together?"

Six months later, they weren't speaking to each other. Their dream brownstone had turned into a nightmare, and their fifteen-year friendship was in shambles.

What went wrong?

The same thing that derails many potential real estate partnerships: They skipped the prenup.

Not the marriage kind—the real estate kind.

Real estate partnerships fail for the same reason many relationships do: people lead with emotion and forget about the business.

I know because I've lived both sides of this story.

At seventeen, I left home and moved twenty-two times in five years. I experienced homelessness and couch-surfing between relatives until I overstayed my welcome. Each move taught me something crucial about real

1

estate: your relationship with housing is the most important relationship you'll ever have.

Working at a bank at nineteen changed my life. Finally, I was learning the language of money, credit, and property. By twenty-nine, as a single mom working purely on commission, I took my first big risk: buying my first property in Brooklyn alone. That purchase taught me I could do it by myself.

But my second property? That taught me I could do even more with the right partner.

I still remember that lunch break with my work bestie. I had spotted my dream brownstone, but the price tag was beyond what I could get approved for. Looking across the table at the one colleague I knew had both the income to qualify and the financial savvy to understand a good deal, I took a chance.

"Want to buy a property together?"

Unlike Kiana and Anthony, we treated this partnership like a business from day one. Clear ownership percentages. A defined timeline for refinancing. When the time came, I refinanced the property. He walked away with a profitable return on his investment, and I got my dream brownstone. Best of all? We're still friends today.

You see, I've spent over two decades watching people fall in and out of love—with properties and with partners. As a former banker turned real estate matchmaker, I've seen thousands of property partnerships succeed brilliantly and fail spectacularly. The difference often comes down to one thing: preparation.

Along the way, I discovered something crucial: The rules of successful property partnerships mirror the rules of successful relationships.

Trust and transparency? That comes from having honest financial conversations before you commit. Shared goals and values? That's about aligning your investment timeline and exit strategy. Clear communication? It's putting everything in writing from day one. Compatible financial habits? Understanding not just what's in someone's bank account but how they handle money. Exit strategy? Just like a prenup, it's not about planning to fail but about protecting everyone's interests.

These aren't just theories. Working in banking taught me the numbers. Being homeless taught me the stakes. And that successful partnership with my colleague taught me the formula.

In today's market, with median home prices in New York hitting $558,000 and the average salary at $62,000, going at it alone isn't just difficult—it's often impossible.

But here's what most people don't realize: Some of the most successful real estate empires were built on partnerships.

This book will show you exactly how to:

- Find partners who complement your financial profile
- Structure deals that protect everyone involved
- Build wealth together while maintaining relationships
- Create generational wealth through strategic partnerships
- Turn housing from a burden into an opportunity

Whether you're:

- A single parent looking for stability
- Young professionals tired of paying sky-high rent
- Friends considering pooling resources
- Family members wanting to build wealth together
- Or anyone seeking a path to property ownership

This book will give you the blueprint to do it right.

Remember Kiana and Anthony? Their story didn't have to end in a broken friendship and shattered dreams. They had all the ingredients for success. They just needed the recipe.

That's what you're holding in your hands right now: a step-by-step guide to finding and creating successful property partnerships. By the time you finish this book, you'll know:

- How to evaluate your partnership readiness
- What to look for in a potential partner
- When to say yes (and when to walk away)
- Where the hidden opportunities lie
- Why some partnerships thrive while others fail
- Most importantly, how to protect yourself and your relationships while building wealth

In the coming chapters, we'll walk through every stage of property partnerships, from first conversation to final closing. You'll hear real stories of successes and failures. You'll get practical tools and templates. And you'll learn how to turn property partnerships from a risky venture into a reliable path to wealth.

Ready to get Pair'D?

Let's begin.

CHAPTER 1

The Profile - Getting Your Shit Together Before You Start Swiping

"The relationship you have with yourself sets the tone for every other relationship you have." – Robert Holden

Know Thyself Before You Partner Up

Preparation is the foundation of success, whether you're embarking on a new relationship or exploring property partnerships. Just as you would create a dating profile to showcase who you are and what you're looking for, crafting your property partnership profile is about presenting your best self—financially and personally.

But here's the catch: instead of agonizing over your best selfie or most clever bio, this process requires something deeper. It's about confronting your financial realities and defining what you truly want in a partnership. While this might feel intimidating, it's an opportunity for you to clarify your goals and values.

Let me introduce you to Sean Watkins. Fresh off a tough divorce, Sean was eager to "get back out there"—not in dating, but in the real estate market. He walked into my office with a steady job, some savings, and a dream of buying a property with someone to share the costs and build equity. However, as we delved into his situation, it became clear that Sean wasn't ready. His unresolved credit card debt from his marriage, inconsistent income from his new commission-based job, and lack of a clear vision for his partnership goals were all red flags.

Sean was making the same mistake many people make when dating: jumping into something new without first understanding himself.

Let me walk you through the process Sean needed to follow to turn things around. These are the same **four essential steps** every aspiring property partner must take to set themselves up for success. Each step builds on the last, helping you move from self-awareness to actionable goals.

Step 1: The Self-Assessment

Before you can be a great partner, you have to know yourself. In real estate, this means taking a hard look at your financial situation and habits. Think of this step as a form of self-care—a way to get yourself into the best possible position before inviting someone else into the equation.

This is about **Internal Locus of Control**—a concept that essentially means taking ownership of your life. It's the belief that your actions, choices, and mindset ultimately determine your outcomes rather than external forces like luck or other people. When it comes to financial partnerships, this mindset is everything. You can't rely on a partner to "save" your financial situation or assume that things will magically work out because you've found someone to share the load.

As Oprah wisely says: *"You are responsible for your own life. If you're waiting for somebody to save you, to fix you, to even help you, you are wasting your time. Only you have the power to move your life forward."* This is not just an inspirational quote—it's a hard truth, especially when money is involved. A partnership, no matter how aligned or promising, will crumble if you aren't clear about your own role and responsibilities.

Taking control means addressing your past financial mistakes, learning from them, and being proactive about your future. It's not about perfection; it's about progress. Whether it's paying down debt, building up savings, or simply understanding where your money is going each month, these steps create a foundation of confidence and readiness. When you take ownership of your financial story, you're no longer at the mercy of circumstances—you're in charge of your journey.

> **Reflection Box:**
> What unresolved financial baggage might you be carrying?
> Are you prepared to be honest about your money habits and patterns?
> What kind of partner are you capable of being at this moment?

Many people think they're ready to partner because they're tired of renting or eager to invest. But rushing in without clarity leads to frustration and unmet expectations. Sean had to go through what I call "financial therapy"—a period of self-reflection where he worked to address his habits, stabilize his income, and create a vision for his future.

Step 2: Getting Real About Money

Talking about money is one of the most challenging conversations to have, even with yourself. For many of us, it's tied to feelings of shame, fear, or anxiety. We avoid it, we justify it, and sometimes, we bury it altogether. But entering a property partnership without financial honesty is like starting a marriage with a lie to make yourself look better. Things might go fine at first, but it won't hold up when the pressure's on.

This is where the **financial strip-down** comes in—a process of peeling back the layers of your financial life to understand where you stand and what you're bringing to the table. It's not about judgment or comparison. It's about honesty and preparation.

Your Financial Strip-Down (see worksheet at): *https://www.pairgap.com*

Think of this process as a way to get naked with your finances. Each layer you examine brings you closer to understanding your true financial picture. Here's how to start:

1. **Check Your Credit Report:**
   Your credit report is like your financial dating history—it tells the story of how you've handled money in the past. It's not just about the score; it's about the story behind it. Are there missed payments? High credit card balances? Outstanding loans? This is your opportunity to understand how lenders (and potential partners) might view you.

   Tip: Use free resources like AnnualCreditReport.com to get a detailed view of your report. Look for errors or outdated information that might be dragging your score down and work to correct them.

2. **Look at Your Debt:**
   Debt is a reality for most people. It is the baggage you bring into any financial partnership, but not all debt is created equal. Some debt, like a mortgage or student loans, can be strategic. But you need to know what's weighing you down and how manageable it is. Are you drowning in high-interest credit card debt? Do you have payment plans that might impact your ability to contribute to a property investment?

   Reflection: Write down every debt you owe, from credit cards to car loans to that $50 you still owe your friend. Seeing it all in one place can feel overwhelming, but it's the first step toward taking control.

3. **Review Your Spending Habits:**
   If your credit report is your financial history, your spending habits are your financial personality. What do your habits say about you? Are you a spender or a saver? Do you track where your money goes, or

do you end up surprised at the end of every month? Understanding your patterns helps you identify areas where you can cut back or reallocate resources to save for a partnership.

Activity: For one month, track every dollar you spend. Categorize it into essentials (housing, utilities, groceries) and non-essentials (dining out, subscriptions, shopping). This exercise can be a real eye-opener.

4. **Examine Your Savings:**

Savings are your safety net—they show your ability to handle unexpected costs and demonstrate financial stability. How much do you have saved for emergencies? Are you setting aside money specifically for a property purchase? This shows that you're prepared to contribute and handle unexpected challenges.

Tip: Aim to have at least three to six months' worth of living expenses saved in an emergency fund before entering a property partnership. Beyond that, start building a dedicated savings account for your investment.

Why This Matters for Partnerships

When you bring unresolved financial baggage into a partnership, it doesn't just affect you—it affects your partner, too. Hidden debts, poor credit, or inconsistent saving habits can create tension and mistrust, making it harder to work together effectively.

Taking the time to get real about your money not only improves your financial standing but also shows potential partners that you're serious, responsible, and prepared.

My Story: Learning the Hard Way

When I was in college, I ran up credit cards like they were Monopoly money, buying things I didn't need and ignoring the consequences. It wasn't until I tried to buy my first car that reality hit me. My credit score was so low that I couldn't qualify for financing. It was humbling, to say the least. But that wake-up call was exactly what I needed. I faced my mistakes, started paying down my debt, and worked on improving my credit. It wasn't easy, but it gave me the confidence and ability to move forward.

The same transformation can happen for you. No one has a perfect financial history, but with awareness and effort, you can take control and position yourself as a strong, reliable partner.

Reflection Questions:
- What's the story your credit report tells?
- Are there any debts you're currently avoiding or not addressing?
- How do your spending habits reflect your financial values?
- Do you have enough savings to handle emergencies or unexpected costs?
- What steps can you take to improve your financial profile over the next three months?

By getting real about your money now, you're laying the foundation for a successful and stress-free property partnership in the future.

Step 3: Defining Your Ideal Match

In dating, knowing what you want and what you don't want is crucial to finding the right partner. Without a clear vision, you risk entering a mismatched partnership that leads to frustration or, worse, financial loss. Let's break this down into three key areas: financial goals, investment style, and property preferences.

Financial Goals

Your financial goals will define the foundation of your partnership. Ask yourself: What do I want to achieve, and how quickly do I want to achieve it? Think of these as the phases of your journey:

- **Short-term Goals (The Dating Phase)**

  Focus on immediate wins, like purchasing a property that can generate rental income within the first year. This might involve investing in a ready-to-rent property that requires minimal renovation or management effort. The goal here is to see quick returns while building your experience.

- **Medium-term Goals (The Going Steady Phase)**

  Your focus shifts to properties you can hold for five to seven years to build equity. For example, a duplex or triplex where you live in one unit and rent out the others can help you build wealth steadily while offsetting your mortgage costs. This phase is about balancing growth and stability.

- **Long-term Goals (The Marriage Phase)**

  This is where the big picture comes into play. Perhaps you aim to own multiple properties that generate enough passive income to support you in retirement or long-term appreciation. Think about larger investments, like multi-family buildings or commercial properties, that generate consistent passive income over decades. This is your "forever home" strategy, but with a focus on financial returns.

Investment Style

Your investment style is like your relationship personality. How much risk are you comfortable taking? Your investment style will dictate the types of properties and partnerships you pursue.

- **Conservative (The Slow and Steady Type)**
  You prefer low-risk investments like turnkey rental properties that are ready to rent out immediately. This approach minimizes stress and focuses on consistent, reliable income. Think about suburban homes or apartments in established markets with steady demand.

- **Moderate (The Balanced Relationship Type)**
  You're open to a mix of safe and slightly risky investments. For instance, purchasing rental properties while taking on some light renovation projects. This style offers a balance between stability and growth. You may target properties that need cosmetic updates to increase their value without major structural changes.

- **Aggressive (The Passionate Romance Type)**
  You're not afraid of high risk if it means high reward. This could involve flipping distressed properties, buying in up-and-coming neighborhoods, or taking on larger renovation projects. This style requires a sharp eye for market trends, confidence, resources, and a tolerance for uncertainty.

Property Preferences

Beyond finances, your preferences for the type of property and its location will play a huge role in narrowing the search for the perfect property and ensuring compatibility with your partner. Here's how to think about them:

- **Location Commitments**
  Decide how far you're willing to venture. Properties within 30 miles of a city center are often ideal for rental demand, but suburban or rural areas may offer lower costs and higher profit margins depending on your strategy.

- **Style Requirements**

  Consider the aesthetic and functional qualities that matter to you. Do you prefer properties with modern designs, historical charm, or unique architectural features? These preferences may seem minor, but they impact the property's appeal to tenants or buyers and its overall marketability.

- **Deal Breakers**

  Just like in dating, deal breakers are non-negotiable. For example, are you open to properties in flood zones, or do you avoid them entirely? What about high property taxes or restrictive zoning laws that could limit your investment potential? Knowing what you won't tolerate will save you time and protect your investment.

By clearly defining your goals, style, and preferences, you'll have a roadmap for selecting the right partner and property. This process also ensures you're not swayed by short-term excitement or external pressure, keeping you focused on what truly aligns with your vision.

When Sean and I worked through his ideal match profile, he realized that he wanted a partnership focused on medium-term goals. He envisioned holding a multi-family property for 5-10 years, building equity steadily with someone who shared his conservative investment style. His preferences were clear: properties close to the city, modern or with local charm, and absolutely no flood zones or significant repair projects.

By defining his goals, investment style, and property preferences, Sean gained clarity and confidence. He was no longer chasing vague ideas—he had a roadmap to guide his decisions and attract the right partner.

Reflection Box:
- What are your short-, medium-, and long-term goals for property investment?
- How much risk are you willing to take in your investments?
- What are your absolute deal breakers when it comes to properties?

Step 4: Packaging Yourself as a Partner

Showcasing Your Strengths

Your strengths are what make you a valuable partner. This could be anything from financial stability to specialized skills or knowledge that would benefit the partnership. Ask yourself:

- Do I have a strong credit history and steady income that demonstrate financial reliability?
- Am I knowledgeable in areas like real estate, construction, or property management?
- Can I contribute capital or secure financing quickly when needed?
- Am I a strategic thinker who excels at planning, organization, and problem-solving?

Take Sean, for example. After months of self-reflection and financial clean-up, Sean was able to confidently highlight his unique strengths. He had a steady income, a solid understanding of rental markets, and a hands-on approach to property upkeep. These attributes made him an appealing partner for someone seeking reliability and active engagement.

Your strengths don't have to be flashy, but they do need to be clear. The key is to articulate how they add value to the partnership.

Understanding Partnership Dynamics

Just as important as what you bring to the table is how you interact with others. Your partnership dynamics reflect your approach to collaboration, decision-making, and problem-solving. This is the heart of what makes partnerships work—or fail.

Some key questions to consider:

- Are you more decisive and action-oriented, or do you prefer a collaborative approach where decisions are made jointly?

- How do you handle conflict or unexpected challenges? Are you calm under pressure and focused on solutions?

- Do you want to be actively involved in day-to-day operations, or do you prefer to delegate responsibilities?

Sean described his style as collaborative but decisive. He valued his partner's input and was open to discussion but wasn't afraid to make tough calls when needed. To keep things running smoothly, he emphasized open communication, setting weekly check-ins, and assigning clear roles to avoid overlap or confusion.

Your style isn't just about how you like to work—it's about creating a rhythm that allows both partners to thrive. By clearly articulating your approach, you set the tone for how you'll navigate challenges and share successes.

Setting Your Boundaries

No partnership can succeed without boundaries. These non-negotiables are the foundation for long-term compatibility, preventing conflicts by ensuring both parties are clear on their expectations from the start.

What are your timelines for buying, holding, or exiting a property? Do you have specific risk tolerances, or are you open to taking calculated risks?

Are there certain property types or locations that are deal-breakers for you? Clarifying these elements early ensures you're aligned with your partner before diving into a major investment.

Sean was particularly clear about his non-negotiables. He required that his partner agree to an exit strategy upfront, understanding that he might want to sell or refinance the property within 5-10 years to pursue other opportunities. By setting this expectation, Sean avoided potential misunderstandings or misaligned goals.

When Sean completed this process, after three months of "dating himself" financially, he had a crystal-clear profile that set him up for success. By addressing his financial weaknesses and improving his credit, Sean not only strengthened his profile but also built the confidence to approach potential partners as a reliable and attractive option.

This clarity allowed Sean to enter the partnership process with purpose. Instead of "selling himself," he was able to articulate his value and find someone whose goals and style matched his own.

Key Takeaways

- **Know Yourself:** Self-awareness and clarity about your strengths and goals form the foundation of your profile.
- **Face Your Finances:** Financial transparency ensures you're ready to partner without surprises or setbacks.
- **Define Your Goals:** A clear vision will help you attract the right partner who aligns with your priorities.
- **Communicate Your Value:** Highlight your unique strengths, style, and boundaries to show why you would be a great partner.

Reflection Questions

- What are the top three strengths you bring to a property partnership?
- How do you prefer to handle decision-making and conflict resolution?
- What are your non-negotiables, and why are they important to you?
- Does your partnership profile align with your short- and long-term goals?

How can you make your profile more appealing to potential partners?

Let's get you ready to step into the dating phase of real estate, where the real magic—and matchmaking—begins!

CHAPTER 2

The Dating Phase – Finding Your Perfect Property Match

"If you want to go fast, go alone.
If you want to go far, go together." – African Proverb

Now that your profile is ready and you've laid the groundwork for partnership, it's time to start your search. Finding the right property might feel like the ultimate goal, but the truth is that the right partner will determine whether your investment succeeds or fails.

It's easy to approach this process with excitement—dreaming about all the possibilities and envisioning how great things could be. But excitement can cloud judgment. People often get swept up in someone's potential, ignore glaring red flags, or rush into commitments because everything feels promising at the start. And just like in romantic relationships, these missteps can lead to regret.

Here's what I've learned after decades of observing property partnerships: **the way you choose your partner matters far more than the property you choose together.** A property can be upgraded, fixed, or even sold off, but the foundation of a strong partnership needs to be rock-solid from the beginning.

First Dates: The Art of Vetting

Choosing a property partner is like entering the dating phase of a relationship. Before you commit, you need to really get to know the person you're considering. This means taking the time to observe their behavior, ask important questions, and pay attention to the details that might not be immediately obvious.

When I partnered with my work bestie, I wasn't going in blind. I already had a solid understanding of his strengths and reliability. Working together gave me firsthand insight into his financial stability—his income was steady, and he managed his money well. Our lunch conversations revealed his financial habits, his goals, and his responsible approach to spending. Beyond that, I had seen his knowledge of real estate and his confidence in decision-making in action.

These weren't lucky guesses or hopeful assumptions—they were observations I made over time. That's what vetting a partner is about: not rushing to conclusions based on a great first impression but taking the time to truly understand who they are and how they operate.

The Importance of Observation

Successful partnerships are built on knowledge, not assumptions. The "honeymoon phase" of any relationship—whether romantic or professional—can be misleading if you only look at surface-level qualities. A person might talk a good game, but their actions over time reveal whether they're truly dependable, aligned with your goals, and prepared to handle challenges.

For example, when considering a partner, look beyond what they say about their finances. How do they act when faced with an unexpected expense? Do they stay calm and organized, or do they panic and deflect responsibility? Observation is your most powerful tool in this phase.

Approach Like a Detective, Not a Dreamer

"What's your credit score?" is the new "What's your sign?"

It's tempting to focus on the potential of a partnership, imagining all the great things you could accomplish together. But this is where many people go wrong—they get caught up in the dream instead of focusing on the reality. Instead, approach this phase with the curiosity of a detective.

Dig deeper than the surface, and don't shy away from potentially awkward topics. Asking tough questions upfront may feel uncomfortable, but it's far better than discovering unpleasant surprises down the road.

Reflection Box:
- What qualities make you trust someone as a partner?
- How can you observe or verify these qualities in real-life situations?
- Are you willing to ask tough questions upfront, even if it feels awkward?

Financial Compatibility: A Non-Negotiable

If property partnerships are a financial marriage, then your financial compatibility is the prenup. Before you make any decisions, you need to understand your potential partner's financial situation in detail.

This isn't about judgment—it's about transparency and alignment. Does your partner have a stable job and manageable debt? Are they committed to financial goals, or are they still figuring things out? Do they have a clear track record of handling money responsibly?

In my experience, people are often more comfortable sharing personal secrets than financial truths. But in a property partnership, financial intimacy comes first. If someone hesitates to disclose their financial reality, that's a red flag.

Tip Box:

- Look for patterns in how your potential partner handles money:
  - Are their credit and payment histories consistent?
  - Do they save for emergencies or take unnecessary risks?
- Be open about your own financial situation and expect the same from them. Transparency goes both ways.

What Truly Matters in a Partnership

It's easy to get excited when you and your potential partner both love the same type of property. But real compatibility goes far deeper than aesthetics. I've seen partnerships with perfect property taste crumble because the partners couldn't agree on the basics: how long to hold the property, how to manage it, or what to do with the profits.

A successful partnership requires alignment in values and goals. Are you both looking for long-term growth, or is one of you focused on flipping for quick profits? Do you have similar risk tolerances? Are you both prepared to be active participants, or is one of you hoping to play a more passive role?

These aren't questions you can skip. They form the foundation of your partnership agreement and guide every decision you'll make together.

Reflection Box:

- Are your investment goals short-term, medium-term, or long-term?
- How do you feel about taking financial risks in this partnership?
- What's your preferred approach to property management—hands-on or hands-off?

The Money Talk: Uncomfortable but Critical

Most people delay having serious money conversations until they're already deep into the process. This is a mistake. The most successful partners tackle the hard conversations upfront before they even start looking at properties.

The money talk isn't just about sharing rough numbers. It's about diving into the details. The mistake most people make is falling in love with a property and then scrambling to figure out how to afford it with their partner. Successful partnerships work the other way around. They start with transparency and honesty about finances before looking at properties.

What does this look like in practice? It means going beyond vague reassurances like "Yeah, I can afford it." It means rolling up your sleeves and diving into the details:

- Reviewing bank statements and credit reports.
- Discussing debt and payment history.
- Talking about where the down payment is coming from.
- Examining income stability and financial commitments.

These questions aren't invasive—they're essential.

If someone isn't willing to be transparent during these conversations, that's a sign of deeper issues. Good partners are open, honest, and willing to confront uncomfortable truths.

Tip Box:
- Approach the money talk with curiosity and respect, not judgment.
- Focus on finding solutions together rather than dwelling on financial shortcomings.

Red Flags and Green Lights

Partnership red flags often reveal themselves early in conversations. Be alert to statements like:

- "We don't need lawyers." *(Yes, you do.)*
- "Let's keep it flexible." *(Translation: I don't want to commit.)*
- "Trust me." *(If they say this more than once, ask for proof.)*
- "We'll figure it out as we go." *(Spoiler: You won't.)*

On the other hand, green lights to look for include partners who come prepared, ask thoughtful questions, and value accountability.

Green Flags in Financial Conversations

- They show up prepared with organized paperwork.
- They ask thoughtful questions about your finances, too.
- They're willing to discuss worst-case scenarios and plan for them.
- They value putting everything in writing to avoid misunderstandings.

What Nobody Tells You

The best partnerships don't begin with fireworks—they begin with clear expectations, mutual respect, and written agreements. The "exciting" partnerships where someone offers an "amazing opportunity" you need to act on right now? Those are usually disasters waiting to happen.

The strongest partners share your values, communicate openly, and stay calm under pressure. They don't promise perfection; they commit to honesty and collaboration.

Reflection Questions
1. What qualities am I looking for in a property partner beyond financial compatibility?
2. Have I had open and honest conversations with my potential partner about priorities and risks?
3. Are there any red flags I'm ignoring because I'm too focused on the opportunity?

Bottom Line

You're not just buying property together; you're entering a financial marriage. The person you choose as your partner will shape your experience and your success. A bad partner can turn a great property into a nightmare, but a good partner can make even an average property a winning investment.

Ready to take the next step? Let's talk about moving from dating to commitment in the next chapter.

CHAPTER 3

Taking It to the Next Level
– Building Trust and
Setting Expectations

"Coming together is a beginning, staying together is progress,
and working together is success." – Henry Ford

Congratulations—you've found a promising partner. That's a significant step, but now the real work begins. It's one thing to identify someone who shares your vision; it's another to structure your relationship in a way that supports long-term success.

This phase is about building trust, defining roles, and putting systems in place to ensure that your partnership thrives. Just like moving from casual dating to a committed relationship, taking your property partnership to the next level requires clear communication, thoughtful planning, and mutual respect.

Let me tell you about Nicole and James. They never shared a home, but they shared something even more important: a vision for financial freedom through real estate. Nicole had impeccable credit, while James had a down payment saved up. Separately, they each faced significant obstacles to homeownership. Together, they turned those obstacles into opportunities.

Their first property purchase was a modest duplex. Nicole lived in one unit, while James managed the rental income from the other. They split responsibilities and profits, treating their partnership like a business. Within three years, they had refinanced the duplex and used the equity to purchase two additional properties. Today, they own three homes, generate passive income, and are on track to achieve their shared financial goals.

Nicole and James didn't stumble into success—they built it. They took the time to align their priorities, establish clear expectations, and structure their partnership in a way that worked for both of them. Their story illustrates that the most successful property partnerships are about more than pooling resources; they're about creating a foundation of trust, accountability, and shared vision.

Rethinking the "American Dream"

Here's a reality check: the traditional "American Dream" of saving for years to buy a home on your own is no longer feasible for many people. With home prices skyrocketing and wages struggling to keep up, going solo often feels impossible.

In cities like New York, where the median home price is $558,000 and the average salary is $62,000, the math simply doesn't work for most individuals. Add in the rising costs of rent, and it's no wonder that homeownership feels out of reach.

But here's the good news: you don't have to do it alone. Property partnerships are transforming how people achieve homeownership and build wealth. By teaming up with the right partner, you can overcome financial barriers, enter the market sooner, and take advantage of opportunities that would be out of reach on your own.

Think about it:

- Paying $3,000 in rent every month? Over three years, that's $108,000 you've spent building someone else's equity.

- Waiting years to save a 20% down payment? Partnering up could cut that timeline in half.

- Hoping to break into the real estate market? A partnership could be your key to opening the door.

Property partnerships aren't just a workaround for high prices—they're a strategic way to build wealth faster and smarter.

Modern Partnerships in Action

Nicole and James's story exemplifies how partnerships can redefine what's possible. But they're far from the only ones rethinking traditional property ownership.

Take The Brooklyn House, a co-living success story that showcases collaboration's power. Three young professionals—a teacher, a nurse, and a tech worker—were paying $2,500 monthly for cramped apartments in Brooklyn. Frustrated with high rents and low savings, they decided to pool their resources and purchase a brownstone together.

Their partnership wasn't just about affordability but about creating a lifestyle supporting their goals while building equity together. Each had a private bedroom and bathroom but shared common areas like the gourmet kitchen, living room, and converted basement coworking space.

What set The Brooklyn House apart more than the structure of their living arrangements was the way they treated their partnership like a business. They created a formal agreement that outlined every aspect of their collaboration, from financial contributions to house rules. They even established a joint bank account for shared expenses and set up a maintenance fund for repairs and upgrades.

The result? Each partner saved $800 a month compared to their previous rent while building equity in a property that was rapidly appreciating in value. They turned a frustrating rental situation into a profitable investment.

Structuring for Success

Every successful partnership—whether it's Nicole and James or The Brooklyn House team—relies on three critical elements: communication, systems, and agreements.

Communication

Open communication is the foundation of any strong partnership. It's not enough to assume that you and your partner are on the same page—you need to confirm it regularly. Schedule check-ins to discuss finances, address concerns, and review your goals. These conversations should be transparent and constructive, creating an environment of trust and accountability.

Nicole and James found that weekly phone calls kept their partnership on track. During these calls, they reviewed rental income, discussed upcoming expenses, and planned for future investments. This consistent communication allowed them to avoid misunderstandings and stay aligned on their goals.

Systems

Strong systems simplify the logistics of property management and reduce the potential for conflict. Whether you're managing the property yourself or hiring a professional manager, having clear processes ensures everyone knows their role and responsibilities.

For Nicole and James, this meant automating rent collection and using property management software to track expenses and profits. The Brooklyn House team hired a cleaning service to handle common areas and set up a maintenance schedule to keep the property in top condition.

Agreements

No matter how much trust exists between partners, a written agreement is essential. This document should clearly outline ownership percentages, management responsibilities, and exit strategies. It's your roadmap for navigating potential challenges and ensuring everyone's interests are protected.

Nicole and James's agreement included provisions for resolving disputes, dividing profits, and selling the property if either partner wanted out. This clarity allowed them to confidently approach their partnership, knowing they were prepared for any eventuality.

Beyond Just Sharing Space

One of the biggest misconceptions about property partnerships is that you must live with your partner or have a personal connection. The truth is the most successful partnerships often operate like businesses. What matters isn't proximity or friendship—it's alignment, professionalism, and mutual respect.

Nicole and James weren't lifelong friends or roommates. What they shared was a commitment to their vision and a willingness to collaborate. By treating their partnership as a professional relationship, they avoided the pitfalls of informal arrangements and built a foundation for long-term success.

The Power of a Shared Vision

A strong partnership doesn't just split costs—it amplifies opportunities. When you partner with the right person, your potential grows exponentially. You can achieve goals faster, share risks and responsibilities, and combine your skills and expertise to make smarter decisions.

Nicole and James's journey shows that partnerships aren't about proximity—they're about purpose. Whether you're living in the same building or managing properties from opposite sides of the country, the key is alignment. Shared vision, mutual respect, and a professional approach are the cornerstones of any successful collaboration.

Key Takeaways

1. Modern partnerships offer flexibility—there's no one-size-fits-all model.
2. Open communication and strong systems are essential for success.
3. Written agreements protect everyone and ensure fairness.
4. Treat your partnership like a business, not a casual arrangement.
5. Focus on shared goals and a clear vision rather than shared space.

Reflection Questions

Ask yourself:

- What type of partnership model aligns with your goals and lifestyle?
- What unique strengths do you bring to a partnership?
- What qualities and contributions do you need in a partner?
- How will you structure your partnership to ensure clarity and accountability?

The Final Word

Taking your property partnership to the next level can feel like a leap of faith, but it's also a leap toward opportunity. The traditional path of waiting to save up alone might work for some, but why wait when you can start building wealth together now?

By finding the right partner, creating strong agreements, and approaching your relationship with purpose, you can unlock opportunities that would be impossible to achieve on your own. Whether you're investing with someone across town or across the country, the key to success is the same: clarity, communication, and collaboration.

CHAPTER 4

A Conversation on the Science of Choosing Your Perfect Property Match

Featuring Arlene Washburn

Science-Based Relationship Coach, Certified Master Executive Matchmaker, and Former CEO of the Matchmaking Institute

"Together Everyone Achieves More." - Nikki Merkerson

When you've built trust and clarified your goals, the next step is finding the right property to bring your vision to life. But what if the secret to a successful property partnership lies in principles drawn from relationship science?

To explore this idea, I sat down with Arlene Washburn, a renowned science-based relationship coach, master executive matchmaker, and former CEO of the only state-licensed school for matchmaking. Arlene has spent years bridging science, research, and human connection to help people build successful personal and professional relationships.

What follows is a candid, eye-opening conversation about how the principles of compatibility, communication, and collaboration apply to property partnerships.

The Prenup Mindset: Setting Boundaries

Nikki: Arlene, let's start with something I hear all the time. People ask, "What happens if things go wrong?" I always emphasize due diligence upfront to prevent problems later. What's your take on creating boundaries in property partnerships?

Arlene: First, let's get a prenup because we're talking about money. Even in personal relationships, I strongly advocate for them when there are significant assets involved. When people are ready to invest, they've usually achieved some financial success they want to protect. And the truth is, nothing's guaranteed. Setting clear boundaries upfront isn't just about protecting what you've built; it's about ensuring that if things don't work out, you can separate cleanly and fairly.

Compatibility: Beyond the Surface

Nikki: Pairgap is built around matching people who are compatible for co-ownership. Compatibility is key, whether someone's buying property with friends, family, or strangers. How does compatibility in co-ownership compare to romantic relationships?

Arlene: There are a lot of parallels. Compatibility in both cases starts with shared core values. For co-owners, that means aligning on key life values like financial outlook, career priorities, and long-term goals. For example, some people see a job as just a way to pay bills, while others are deeply passionate about their careers. These perspectives shape how you approach financial planning and investment. If one partner is a spender and the other is a saver, there's bound to be conflict. It's vital to identify these differences early and ensure alignment.

The Science of Vetting: Asking the Right Questions

Nikki: I always advise asking tough questions upfront to really understand who you're partnering with. But sometimes, people feel awkward about this. What's your advice for navigating those conversations?

Arlene: People often lead with emotions, which can cloud their judgment. The key is to separate emotions from logic early on. Ask the big questions before you're too invested: What are their financial goals? How do they handle conflict? What's their long-term vision?

But how you ask matters. Instead of bombarding someone with direct questions, use storytelling or open-ended scenarios. For example, ask, "How would you handle an unexpected repair that costs $10,000?" This approach fosters dialogue rather than defensiveness and helps you get to the heart of someone's values without making it feel like an interrogation.

Conflict: A Tool for Growth

Nikki: Conflict is inevitable in any partnership. How do you ensure it's productive rather than destructive?

Arlene: Conflict is a way to uncover differences and build understanding— it's not inherently bad. The issue is how people handle it. Do you fight fair, or do you hit below the belt? Productive conflict is about finding compromise or agreeing to disagree without crossing lines of disrespect. For property partnerships, this means establishing ground rules for communication and decision-making.

The Shared Economy: Collaboration as the Future

Nikki: We're seeing a trend toward collaboration in every area, from Airbnb to co-living. How does the shared economy influence the way we approach partnerships?

Arlene: Collaboration is the future. In the past, marriage was often the primary form of collaboration outside of traditional business partnerships. Today, people are pooling resources in new ways. Major investors, for example, rarely use only their own money—they pool resources to achieve bigger goals. The same applies to property partnerships.

When people collaborate, they can reach their goals faster and reduce individual risk. Whether it's a romantic partner, a friend, or a stranger, the shared economy has taught us that pooling resources and skills creates opportunities that wouldn't exist otherwise.

The Power of the Real Estate Prenup

Nikki: At Pairgap, we emphasize creating what I call a "real estate prenup." It's a way to plan for the "what ifs" before they happen. Why do you think these agreements are so important?

Arlene: A prenup, whether in marriage or business, isn't about expecting failure—it's about being prepared. It's like having health insurance. You hope you never need it, but if you do, it's there to protect you. A real estate prenup clarifies how to dissolve a partnership if needed, whether that's through buyouts, selling, or bringing in new partners.

Having these agreements in place minimizes conflict and protects everyone's interests. It's about ensuring that even in the worst-case scenario, the relationship ends cleanly and respectfully.

Key Takeaways

1. **Plan for Success:** Boundaries and agreements protect both parties and set the stage for a productive partnership.
2. **Focus on Compatibility:** Core values and long-term goals matter more than surface traits.
3. **Embrace Collaboration:** The shared economy has shown us that working together achieves better results.

4. Address Conflict Head-On: Clear communication and established boundaries turn challenges into opportunities.

Reflection Questions
- What are your core values, and how do they align with a potential partner's?
- How will you handle disagreements or unexpected challenges?
- What are your financial goals, and how do they shape your vision for a partnership?
- Are you prepared to discuss and establish boundaries before committing?

About Arlene Washburn

Arlene Washburn is an award-winning expert in matchmaking and relationships, recognized as the most innovative woman in the matchmaking industry. She is a passionate advocate for ethical matchmaking and the founder of the **Love Pro Mastermind Academy**, where she trains both aspiring and experienced matchmakers. Through her academy, Arlene equips professionals with the tools and strategies needed to succeed in modern matchmaking.

In addition to her educational efforts, Arlene serves as the **Managing Director of the Worldwide Referral Network**, a global platform connecting matchmaking professionals and fostering collaboration across the industry. She is also the host of the **Matchmaker Mentor Podcast**, where she shares her insights on matchmaking, relationships, and personal growth.

With her science-based approach and commitment to innovation, Arlene continues to shape the future of matchmaking and help individuals build meaningful, lasting connections.

The Final Word

As Arlene so beautifully put it: *"What we say and what we do comes from what we believe. If your beliefs aren't supporting your goals, that's what needs to change."*

Partnerships aren't just about splitting costs—they're about aligning values, communicating effectively, and building a shared vision. Whether you're entering a property partnership or a lifelong relationship, the principles remain the same: plan thoughtfully, communicate openly, and collaborate for success.

Ready to structure your partnership? In the next chapter, we'll outline creating agreements that support your goals and protect your investment.

CHAPTER 5

Location, Location, Location – A New World Emerging

*"The world is changing; we must change with it
or risk being left behind."* - Nikki Merkerson

A Smooth Transition

In the previous chapter, we explored the principles of compatibility, communication, and collaboration, drawing insights from relationship science to strengthen property partnerships. Now that you've built trust and clarified your goals, it's time to focus on where this vision comes to life: the perfect location.

Even with the ideal partner and a solid plan, location remains one of the most critical factors in real estate. The right location can amplify the potential of your investment, while the wrong one can leave you struggling to stay afloat. But this isn't just about finding a "hot" neighborhood—it's about understanding the transformative shifts happening in how we live, work, and interact with our environments.

The Future is Closer Than You Think

Let me introduce you to a concept that's reshaping cities around the world: the **fifteen-minute city.**

Imagine living in a place where everything you need is just a fifteen-minute walk or bike ride away:

- Your favorite coffee shop

- Your local grocery store

- A nearby gym

- Your office (if you still go to one)

- Your kid's school

- The restaurant where you celebrate milestones

Sounds like a luxury, right? Yet, this isn't a far-off fantasy—it's happening right now in cities across America and beyond. Urban planners are prioritizing livability and accessibility, creating neighborhoods where convenience and community thrive. And here's the kicker: smart investors are paying attention and positioning themselves early to benefit from these changes.

The New Gold Rush: Zoomtowns

Remember when living near your office was a non-negotiable? Those days are over. The rise of remote work has given birth to **Zoomtowns**—areas experiencing rapid growth as remote workers seek out affordable, lifestyle-friendly locations.

These aren't just trends; they're seismic shifts in how we live. Cities and towns that were once overlooked are now flourishing because they offer the quality of life people want—without the price tag of major urban centers.

Take a moment to imagine this: A sleepy town in the mountains with great Wi-Fi suddenly sees an influx of young professionals, tech startups, and vibrant community spaces. Property values soar, local businesses thrive, and a new kind of economic boom emerges.

"But how do you know which areas will take off?"

The Smart Investor's Guide to Location

Successful investing in this new world isn't about following the hype—it's about understanding the data. Let's break it down into three key focus areas:

1. Digital Infrastructure

- High-speed internet coverage is non-negotiable for remote workers.
- Look for areas attracting tech companies or fostering remote work initiatives.
- Analyze remote work statistics to identify growth areas.

2. Community Features

- Check walkability scores—highly walkable neighborhoods attract premium buyers and renters.
- Green spaces aren't just nice to have; they're essential for livability and property value.
- Cultural amenities like museums, theaters, and unique dining experiences indicate a thriving community.
- Assess local business growth as a sign of economic health.

3. Future Development

- Track transit plans—new transit lines can transform a neighborhood overnight.
- Research zoning changes that allow for mixed-use developments.
- Look at new construction permits and announcements of major employer relocations.

A Case Study in Smart Investing

Last year, a client of mine was eager to buy in a "hot" neighborhood everyone was buzzing about. But when we analyzed the data, the numbers told a different story. A smaller, less talked-about area nearby showed far more promise:

- A new transit line was in the works.

- Zoning changes were opening opportunities for mixed-use developments.

- Three major employers were moving to the area.

- Plans for a park and community center were underway.

Despite initial skepticism, they trusted the data and purchased in the overlooked neighborhood. One year later, their property value had increased by 20%, while the "hot" neighborhood had plateaued.

How to Identify the Next Big Thing

Here's what I tell every investor: the future belongs to those who pay attention to trends and take calculated risks. Use this checklist to guide your location research:

1. **Follow the Infrastructure:**
   - Where are new transit lines being built?
   - Are digital connectivity upgrades happening?
   - Are new schools or community centers being constructed?

2. **Watch the Innovation:**
   - Which areas are attracting tech companies and creative businesses?
   - Where are entrepreneurs setting up shop?
   - Are coworking spaces and startup hubs popping up?

3. **Track the Lifestyle Shifts:**
   - Are walkability scores improving?
   - Are there new parks, bike lanes, or recreational spaces?
   - Are local governments embracing sustainable development?

Reflection Questions

1. What lifestyle trends or community features matter most to you and your partners?
2. How does this location align with your long-term investment strategy?
3. What infrastructure developments (like transit lines or tech hubs) could influence the area's value?
4. What unique opportunities or risks does this location present compared to others?

The Bottom Line

The world is changing, and the real estate market is changing with it. The days of blindly following hype are over. Smart investors know that **location matters differently now**—it's about how people want to live, work, and play in a world transformed by technology and shifting priorities.

Are you prepared to adapt? To not just witness the future but actively shape it?

In the next chapter, we'll explore actionable strategies for making these opportunities work for you and your partners. It's not just about finding the right location—it's about leveraging it to build a stronger financial future together.

CHAPTER 6

Shacking Up – Sharing is Caring

"Sharing is Caring- but smart sharing creates success ." — Nikki Merkerson

Collaboration is more than pooling resources. It allows you to gain access to opportunities you might not achieve alone. In today's housing market, where prices are skyrocketing and income growth isn't keeping pace, collaboration can be the key to unlocking neighborhoods, properties, and opportunities that might otherwise be out of reach. By combining efforts and resources, buyers can amplify their buying power and navigate the barriers to homeownership together.

In this chapter, we'll dive deeper into how co-ownership can be a game-changer for accessing housing, break down what it takes to qualify for a mortgage, and explore the numbers behind increased buying power. Let's uncover how the "3 C's" of mortgage qualification—Credit, Capacity, and Collateral—can work in your favor when you collaborate.

Sharing is Caring

After dating someone for a while, things often start to get more serious. You make plans, dream together, and start building a stronger sense of security. The same concept applies to property partnerships. You can dream about homeownership all you want, but without clear conversations and actionable plans, those dreams stay in your head.

For many, the thought of planning for the future—especially financially—is terrifying. What if things go wrong? What if the plan doesn't work out? But here's the thing: the future is coming, whether we're ready or not. Wouldn't you rather step into it prepared?

The Barriers to Homeownership: A Changing Reality

Today's young adults face challenges that make homeownership feel like an impossible goal. The American Dream of owning a home—a cornerstone of wealth-building—seems increasingly out of reach. Rising student debt, stagnant wages, skyrocketing property prices, and a housing market that often feels rigged against first-time buyers have created significant obstacles.

Consider this:

- In the last decade, residential rents have risen 150%, far outpacing income growth.

- The median home price in cities like New York is $558,000, requiring a down payment of over $110,000—an amount that takes decades for the average earner to save.

- The typical homeowner has a net worth of $195,000, compared to just $5,400 for the average renter.

These realities have left many feeling stuck. Renting drains financial resources that could otherwise build equity, while buying solo can feel unattainable.

The Case for Co-Ownership

Enter co-ownership: a solution for those who want to bypass these barriers and build wealth sooner. By teaming up, buyers can:

- Increase Buying Power: Combined incomes allow buyers to qualify for larger loans and access better properties.

- Share Costs: Splitting down payments, monthly mortgage payments, and maintenance expenses makes ownership more affordable.

- Mitigate Risk: Shared responsibility reduces the burden on any one individual, creating a safety net for unexpected challenges.

Understanding Mortgage Math: The 3 C's of Qualification

Let's break down what it takes to qualify for a mortgage. Lenders evaluate borrowers based on three key factors:

1. Credit (Your Financial Trustworthiness)

Your credit score is a snapshot of how well you've managed debt in the past. A strong credit score indicates reliability, while a poor score can lead to higher interest rates or loan denials.

- Why It Matters: A high credit score lowers your interest rate, saving you thousands over the life of your loan.

- How Co-Ownership Helps: If one co-buyer has excellent credit, it can balance out a partner with a weaker score, improving your overall profile.

2. Capacity (Your Ability to Repay)

Lenders assess your income and existing debts to calculate your debt-to-income (DTI) ratio. Ideally, your total debts—including your mortgage payment—shouldn't exceed 43% of your income.

- Why It Matters: A lower DTI ratio signals to lenders that you can comfortably manage your mortgage payments.

- How Co-Ownership Helps: Combined incomes lower the DTI ratio, making the application more attractive to lenders.

3. Collateral (The Property as Security)

The property you're buying acts as collateral for the loan. Lenders want assurance that the property's value justifies the loan amount.

- Why It Matters: A larger down payment reduces the loan-to-value (LTV) ratio, making the loan less risky for lenders.

- How Co-Ownership Helps: Pooling savings allows co-buyers to make larger down payments, improving loan terms and reducing monthly payments.

The Numbers Behind Collaboration

Let's look at how co-ownership changes the game.

- Scenario 1: Buying Solo
  - Income: $75,000/year
  - Max Loan Approval: $300,000
- Scenario 2: Co-Ownership
  - Combined Income: $150,000/year
  - Max Loan Approval: $600,000

By teaming up, buyers double their purchasing power, gaining access to properties in better neighborhoods with higher potential for equity growth.

The Long-Term Benefits of Homeownership

Owning a home isn't just about having a place to live—it's about building wealth. Each mortgage payment builds equity, which acts like a forced savings account. Over time, that equity can be used to:

- Start a business

- Pay off student loans

- Fund retirement
- Reinvest in additional properties

The Collaboration Effect

When you combine forces with a trusted partner, you're not just splitting costs—you're multiplying opportunities. Together, you can:

- Afford homes in desirable neighborhoods.
- Access better loan terms.
- Share responsibilities and risks.

Collaboration opens doors to areas and opportunities that might otherwise remain closed. It's not just about getting into the market—it's about thriving in it.

Reflection Questions
1. What barriers have kept you from pursuing homeownership?
2. How could partnering with someone change your buying power or location options?
3. Are you prepared to have open, honest conversations about finances with a potential partner?
4. What steps can you take today to improve your credit, capacity, or savings?

The Bottom Line

In today's housing market, collaboration isn't just a convenience—it's a necessity. By pooling resources, sharing responsibilities, and working toward common goals, co-ownership creates a path to homeownership that's accessible, sustainable, and rewarding.

Understanding the numbers is key. In the next chapter, we sit down with a lending advisor to break down how co-buyers can qualify together and make smarter financing moves.

CHAPTER 7

A Conversation on Co-Buying

Featuring Jason Gajraj

Insights from a Senior Home Lending Advisor

"Co-buying isn't just about sharing a mortgage; it's about sharing a vision for financial growth and mutual success." — Nikki Merkerson

When it comes to understanding the mortgage process for co-buyers, there's no better guide than Jason Gajraj. With 16 years of experience as a Senior Home Lending Advisor, Jason has helped countless buyers navigate everything from FHA and VA loans to jumbo mortgages. Based in New York City, he specializes in preapproval, low-to-moderate income lending programs, and first-time homebuyer assistance. His ability to demystify complex lending processes has made him a trusted resource for homebuyers of all kinds, including co-buyers.

In this conversation, Jason provides invaluable insights into how the preapproval process works for co-buyers, the role of deeds and notes, and why the bank only cares about numbers—not personal relationships.

The Interview

Nikki: Jason, you've been in the lending industry for over 16 years. With co-buying becoming a growing trend, is the preapproval process for co-buyers different from that of a single buyer?

Jason: That's a great question, Nikki. The short answer is no—the preapproval process for co-buyers is essentially the same as it is for any other borrower. As a lender, we look at the combined income, assets, and credit profiles of all applicants. The goal is to assess their ability to repay the loan, and from our perspective, it doesn't matter if you're buying with a spouse, a friend, or a business partner.

The only difference might be that co-buyers should have clear agreements upfront about who is contributing what—whether it's the down payment, monthly payments, or other costs. While a legally binding document isn't required for preapproval, it's strongly recommended. Having everything outlined helps avoid confusion later and ensures everyone is on the same page. We can then arrange the preapproval accordingly.

Nikki: That's reassuring for many people. Let's talk about ownership structure. Can someone be on the deed without being on the mortgage?

Jason: Absolutely. The person—or people—on the mortgage are the ones responsible for repaying the loan. However, ownership is determined by the deed. You can have someone listed as an owner on the deed without them being on the mortgage. This is often the case when one party is contributing financially, but they want to ensure ownership rights are shared with another person, such as a family member or partner.

It's important to note, though, that if you're on the mortgage, you *must* also be on the deed. This is because the deed secures the lender's interest in the property.

Nikki: That makes sense. Speaking of ownership, what happens if one co-buyer wants to exit the arrangement?

Jason: If a co-buyer wants to step away, the remaining co-owners must refinance the mortgage. This essentially replaces the existing loan with a new one, removing the departing party from the mortgage and, if necessary, the deed.

During this process, the remaining co-buyers must requalify for the loan based on their updated financial profiles. If their income and assets don't meet the lender's requirements, they may need to bring in a new co-buyer to share the financial responsibility.

Nikki: Let's shift gears and talk about co-buying under a business entity, like an LLC. Is that process more complicated?

Jason: Buying under an LLC adds a few extra steps, but it's very manageable. At Chase, we have the ability to close loans in the name of an LLC, which not all lenders offer.

For example, we'll require documentation like the LLC's Articles of Organization, a Certificate of Good Standing issued by the state, and an LLC Resolution outlining how the property will be managed. It's critical to ensure the LLC is in good financial standing. If the LLC has been active for a while, we may also request tax returns to confirm there's no negative income reported.

While the deed can be held by the LLC, the mortgage itself is still tied to the individuals, meaning the repayment responsibility—and reporting to credit agencies—affects personal credit, not business credit.

Nikki: That's a common misconception, isn't it? Many people think that buying under an LLC shields their personal credit. Can you clarify why that's not the case?

Jason: Absolutely. The key point is that a mortgage is a personal promise to repay the loan. Even if the property is held in an LLC, the individuals backing the loan are responsible for the payments.

Some people assume that because the property is under a business entity, it won't affect their personal credit. That's not true. Lenders report mortgage repayment activity to personal credit agencies. The bank focuses on the individuals' ability to repay, not just the business entity's financials.

Nikki: One last question, Jason. Why doesn't the bank care about personal relationships between co-buyers?

Jason: Because relationships don't repay loans—numbers do. The bank's only concern is whether the co-buyers can collectively meet the financial obligations of the mortgage. We evaluate the hard data: credit scores, income, assets, and debt.

Whether you're buying with your spouse, a friend, or a business partner, the relationship dynamics are irrelevant as long as the financials add up. That said, I always advise co-buyers to have clear agreements and open communication. It makes the process smoother for everyone.

Key Takeaways

1. **Preapproval Process:** The preapproval process for co-buyers is no different from that of single buyers. Lenders evaluate combined income, assets, and creditworthiness.

2. **Deed and Mortgage Relationship:** You can be on the deed without being on the mortgage, but if you're on the mortgage, you must be on the deed.

3. Refinancing for Buyouts: If a co-buyer wants out, the remaining partners must refinance the mortgage and requalify based on updated financials.
4. LLC Ownership: While a property can be held in an LLC, the mortgage repayment responsibility remains tied to the individuals and impacts their personal credit.
5. Bank Perspective: Lenders only care about the financial ability to repay the loan, not the personal dynamics between co-buyers.

Reflection Questions

- Are you clear on your financial contributions and responsibilities as a co-buyer?
- How will you navigate the process if one partner wants to exit the arrangement?
- If you're using an LLC, have you prepared all necessary documentation upfront?

Jason's expertise highlights that while co-buying involves a few unique considerations, the process is straightforward with proper planning and preparation. Understanding these key concepts can make all the difference in creating a successful partnership.

CHAPTER 8

The Power of Leverage

"Sometimes the perfect match isn't about chemistry
- it's about leverage." — Nikki Merkerson

As Jason explained in the previous chapter, the foundation of a successful mortgage process is all about aligning the numbers—your income, credit, and assets. But what comes next? How do you take that approval and turn it into a strategic advantage?

This is where leverage comes into play. More than just securing a loan, leverage is about using your property—and your partnership with co-buyers—as a launchpad for building wealth. By treating your property like a business and your co-buyers like partners, you can maximize every dollar, increase your cash flow, and set the stage for long-term financial freedom.

Leverage: Your Key to Scaling Success

Leverage is the ability to amplify your resources to achieve greater results, and in real estate, it's a game-changer. When paired with the collaborative power of co-buying, leverage becomes the ultimate strategy for accessing opportunities that might otherwise be out of reach.

In this chapter, we'll examine how to make the most of your resources, treat your property like a business, and view your lender as an essential part of your team. Let's explore how to turn your property into a wealth-building machine that works for you and your partners.

As we transition from Jason Gajraj's insights into the nuts and bolts of co-buying and lending, it's time to zoom out and explore the bigger picture—how real estate is more than just a financial investment; it's a strategic play fueled by leverage, cash flow, and the potential for long-term wealth building.

Leverage is at the heart of every successful real estate deal, whether you're a first-time buyer or a seasoned investor. Jason emphasized the importance of building a team, with the lender as a key player in achieving financial goals. But how does leverage tie into all of this, and why is it so addictive for those who get started?

What Is Leverage and Why Is It Powerful?

Leverage allows you to do more with less. It's the art of using borrowed money to amplify your purchasing power and investment returns. Instead of saving for years to buy a property outright, you can put down a fraction of the cost, secure a mortgage, and let your investment grow while you pay it off.

For example, imagine buying a $500,000 property. Without leverage, you'd need $500,000 in cash. With leverage, you might only need $50,000 for a down payment. The property appreciates in value, builds equity, and generates cash flow, all while requiring significantly less upfront capital from you.

The Home Becomes the Business

Think of your home not just as a place to live but as a business in itself. The mortgage becomes a predictable operating expense, and the property becomes a revenue-generating asset.

As Jason mentioned in his interview, lenders evaluate your financial profile and your ability to repay the loan—not your personal relationship with a co-buyer. They focus on whether the numbers work, and this is where leverage becomes a game-changer. The more strategic you are about structuring your finances and property, the more opportunities you can create.

Key benefits of leveraging your home as a business:

- Equity Growth: Each mortgage payment builds your equity, which can later be tapped into for future investments.

- Cash Flow Opportunities: Renting out part of the property or leveraging additional units creates monthly income.

- Tax Benefits: Mortgage interest and property expenses often provide tax advantages.

The Role of the Lender as Part of Your Team

Lenders don't just approve loans; they're critical partners in your investment strategy. Jason highlighted how a skilled lender can help you structure your financing to maximize leverage and cash flow.

By working with a lender who understands your goals, you can:

1. **Secure the Right Loan:** Tailored to your needs and aligned with your strategy.

2. **Plan for Growth:** Use equity and cash flow to position yourself for future investments.

3. **Mitigate Risk:** Ensure your loan terms and cash flow can weather market fluctuations.

A lender isn't just evaluating you—they're working with you to create a sustainable pathway to financial independence.

Why Real Estate Investment Becomes Addictive

There's a reason real estate investors often say, "Once you start, you can't stop." The combination of leverage, cash flow, and equity growth creates a cycle of opportunities that's hard to resist.

Here's how the cycle works:

1. **Leverage Gets You Started:** Your first property builds equity.

2. **Equity Opens Doors:** That equity can be tapped to purchase additional properties.

3. **Cash Flow Fuels Growth:** Rental income or appreciation funds future investments.

4. **Momentum Compounds:** Each property adds to your portfolio, increasing financial stability and wealth.

Understanding Leverage and Risk

Leverage is a double-edged sword. While it can amplify returns, it also magnifies losses if not managed carefully. Jason noted in his interview that banks focus on your ability to repay the loan because they're taking on risk alongside you.

Key considerations when using leverage:

- **Don't Overextend:** Ensure you can afford payments even in challenging market conditions.

- **Build a Cushion:** Maintain liquidity to handle unexpected expenses.

- **Think Long-Term:** Use leverage to create stability and growth, not just quick wins.

Financial Independence Through Leverage and Cash Flow

Financial independence isn't just about paying off your mortgage—it's about creating recurring income streams that allow you to live on your terms.

By leveraging your home as an asset and building cash flow, you can:

- Fund your next investment.

- Start a business.

- Achieve freedom from traditional employment.

Reflection Questions

1. How can you strategically use leverage to achieve your financial goals?

2. Are you maximizing the cash flow potential of your property?

3. How can your lender help you build a sustainable investment strategy?

4. What's your long-term vision for financial independence, and how does leverage fit into it?

The Bottom Line

Leverage isn't just a financial tool—it's the key to turning homeownership into entrepreneurship. By thinking of your home as a business and your lender as a teammate, you can create a pathway to wealth that extends far beyond your first property.

Now that you've learned how to maximize your leverage and treat your property like a business, it's time to protect what you're building. In the next chapter, we'll dive into how to safeguard your investment and partnership through smart legal planning. Because in real estate—just like in life— growth without protection can be risky.

CHAPTER 9

Due Diligence – A Conversation about Protecting Your Partnership

Featuring Sabine Franco

Real Estate Attorney and Founder of Ambitious Legacy Firm

"Never let your emotions overpower your intelligence." - Nikki Merkerson

Entering into co-ownership is a significant decision—one that requires a clear framework and careful planning to protect both the partnership and the investment. Just as a marriage benefits from a well-thought-out prenuptial agreement, co-buyers need a comprehensive plan to protect their investment and partnership.

A strong co-ownership agreement is your prenup for real estate. It sets boundaries, aligns expectations, and provides a roadmap for navigating challenges.

The idea of buying property together can feel risky. Many people shy away from co-buying because they fear the "what-ifs, but with the right safeguards in place, more people may realize that shared ownership is a powerful path to homeownership and wealth-building.

I sat down with real estate attorney **Sabine Franco**, founder of Ambitious Legacy Firm, to discuss how proper due diligence can make co-ownership accessible and secure for more people. Sabine has helped countless clients structure agreements that protect both relationships and investments. As she puts it:

"You should want to protect what you've built. It's only right to safeguard your credit and personal interests. Think of it like a marriage—you're putting a lot on the line, but you can do it in a safe way."

Her approach to due diligence is about preparation, not pessimism—a mindset that can open the door for more people to embrace the concept of co-ownership with confidence.

Why Due Diligence Matters

Nikki: *Sabine, many of the challenges I see in co-ownership arise when people skip the due diligence process. Why is this step so critical?*

Sabine: Due diligence is essential because it establishes a foundation of trust, transparency, and preparation, helping to avoid unnecessary conflict.

Without due diligence, even the strongest partnerships can crumble under pressure. For example, 'What happens if one of us wants to sell? What if someone stops paying their share? What if there's a dispute?' These conversations might be uncomfortable, but having them upfront is far less stressful than dealing with these issues later without a plan. A detailed agreement protects both your financial investment and your relationship.

Details Matter

- **Financial Transparency:** Ensure all parties have a clear understanding of each other's financial situations, including credit scores, income, and outstanding debts.

- **Compatibility Check:** Beyond finances, assess your partner's level of responsibility, communication style, and long-term goals to ensure alignment.

- **Scenario Planning:** Think through various "what if" situations— such as job loss, market downturns, or disagreements over property use—and create contingency plans.

LLCs: The Foundation for Real Estate Partnerships

Nikki: *One of the most common questions I get is about LLCs versus personal ownership. Can you break down why someone might choose an LLC?*

Sabine: An LLC is a smart move for co-buyers and provides an added layer of protection. It limits personal liability—meaning your personal assets won't be at risk if there's an issue with the property. Additionally, it offers tax benefits, like deductions for expenses related to managing the property. You're essentially running the property like a business, which is a mindset shift co-buyers need.

Plus, an LLC formalizes the partnership. The operating agreement acts as a playbook, defining roles, responsibilities, and exit strategies. This is invaluable if someone wants to leave the partnership or if life circumstances change. With an LLC, transitions are smoother, and conflicts are minimized.

Ownership Structures: Joint Tenancy vs. Tenancy in Common

Nikki: *When it comes to ownership structures, what are the options, and how should co-buyers decide?*

Sabine: The right structure depends on your goals, but the two most common options for co-buyers are:

1. **Tenancy in Common (TIC)**
   - **Flexible Ownership:** Each person owns a percentage of the property, which doesn't have to be equal (e.g., 60/40 or 70/30).
   - **Inheritance Options:** You can designate heirs to inherit your share of the property, making it ideal for those who want control over their equity.

2. **Joint Tenancy with Rights of Survivorship (JTWROS)**
   - **Automatic Succession:** If one co-owner passes away, their share automatically transfers to the surviving co-owner(s), bypassing probate. However, this means the deceased cannot leave their share to heirs or designate beneficiaries, as it goes directly to the other owner(s).

When deciding between **Joint Tenancy with Rights of Survivorship** and **Tenancy in Common**, it's essential to consider your goals:

If **inheritance planning** and the ability to leave your share to heirs are priorities, **Tenancy in Common** is the better option.

If **avoiding probate** and ensuring a smooth, automatic transfer of ownership to co-owners is more important, **Joint Tenancy** may be the right choice.

Details to Consider

- Discuss future plans for the property, including inheritance preferences.
- Align the ownership structure with each partner's financial contributions.

Addressing Missed Payments

Nikki: *One of the biggest fears people have is, 'What happens if my partner stops paying?' How can this be handled?*

Sabine: Missed payments are a legitimate concern and can strain any partnership, but they don't have to lead to conflict. Include clauses in your agreement that incentivize accountability, such as:

- **Equity Adjustment:** If one partner stops contributing, their ownership share decreases proportionally while the paying partner's share increases.

- **Buyout Options:** If missed payments persist, the paying partner has the right to buy out the other partner's share at an agreed-upon valuation.

These mechanisms create a sense of fairness and motivate partners to fulfill their obligations.

Details to Include

- Clearly define thresholds for equity adjustments or buyouts.
- Establish timelines for addressing missed payments to avoid prolonged disputes.

Planning for Life's Unexpected Events

Nikki: *Life happens—marriage, divorce, death, even bankruptcy. How can co-buyers plan for these scenarios?*

Sabine: We address life events through proactive legal agreements that protect everyone involved. Key provisions include:

- **Right of First Refusal:** If one partner wants to sell, the other has the first opportunity to buy their share.

- **Transfer Restrictions:** Limit who can become a co-owner to ensure compatibility with the existing partner.

- **Succession Planning:** Outline what happens to ownership shares if a partner passes away. This avoids surprises like inheriting a new co-owner you didn't choose.

Details to Address

- Include provisions for unexpected events like divorce, financial hardship, or major disagreements.
- Regularly update the agreement to reflect changes in circumstances.

Strangers vs. Friends: What's Riskier?

Nikki: *People assume it's riskier to co-own with a stranger than with a friend or family member. What's your take?*

Sabine: Not necessarily. Familiarity can sometimes cloud judgment. Strangers often respect boundaries and agreements more because they don't bring history or assumptions into the partnership. Whether you're partnering with someone you know or a stranger, the key is evaluating their responsibility, compatibility, and credibility—not the nature of your relationship.

Once your names are on the deed, you're financially tied to each other. Their financial habits, legal troubles, or poor decisions can directly impact your credit, the property, and your overall financial health. This is why it's critical to establish clear agreements and conduct due diligence up front—trust is important, but preparation and legal safeguards are essential.

Knowledge is Power: Use the insights you've gained through this process, and don't hesitate to leverage professional expertise. Whether you're working with an attorney, financial advisor, or real estate expert; informed decisions protect your investment and set the stage for a successful partnership.

Protecting Your Partnership

Nikki: *Some people think they don't need an attorney when buying with family or friends. What's your perspective?*

Sabine: An attorney is crucial because co-ownership is a legally binding relationship. Once your names are on the deed, you're financially tied to each other. Their financial habits, legal troubles, or poor decisions can impact you directly.

An attorney helps you navigate these risks by drafting agreements that address potential challenges upfront. Think of it as an investment in protecting your investment.

Details Matter:

- Choose an attorney with experience in real estate and co-ownership agreements.

- Prioritize clarity and thoroughness in your agreements to avoid disputes down the line.

Balancing Risk and Reward

As the conversation with Sabine unfolded, I reflected on my own approach to risk, which I call the **R.I.S.K. Framework**:

- **R – Research:** Gather facts, not assumptions. Know what you're getting into.

- **I – Intuition:** Trust your gut, but back it with data.

- **S – Strategy:** Map out your goals and contingency plans.

- **K – Knowledge:** Use what you've learned to make informed decisions.

Risk tolerance sits at the intersection of your comfort zone and your dreams. Calculated risks pave the way to opportunity, while blind leaps invite unnecessary challenges.

Key Takeaways

- **Plan for the Future:** Due diligence and legal agreements are essential for navigating the complexities of co-ownership.
- **Choose the Right Structure:** Align your ownership structure with your financial goals and long-term plans.
- **Prepare for the Unexpected:** Build provisions for life events, missed payments, and partnership changes into your agreement.
- **Seek Legal Guidance:** An experienced attorney is your best resource for creating a secure and successful partnership.

Final Word

Sabine put it best: *"If you can't get on the same page now, you certainly won't be able to later."*

Due diligence isn't about distrust—it's about preparation. Protecting your partnership with thoughtful planning ensures that challenges are met with solutions, not conflict. The effort you invest now paves the way for a secure and successful co-ownership experience.

CHAPTER 10

Your Legacy – From First
Date to Forever

*"The best relationships aren't about the perfect match—
they're about building something that lasts."* - Nikki Merkerson

Now that you've established partnerships and started building wealth, let's focus on creating something that lasts. Finding the right property partner, ensuring compatibility, and laying the groundwork for trust and shared goals are the first steps. But the real story—the one that lasts beyond you—begins with ensuring your legacy is secure for generations to come.

Building wealth through real estate is an exciting and rewarding journey, but it doesn't end with acquiring properties. Legacy-building goes beyond accumulating assets; it's about ensuring the systems, knowledge, and values are in place to preserve and grow what you've started.

The partnerships and investments you've made aren't just for today; they're the foundation for something much greater. Imagine the excitement of your first property match multiplied across generations—a story of growth, resilience, and opportunity that continues long after you're gone.

The Talk Nobody Wants to Have

Much like those pivotal "relationship status" conversations, there's a discussion you need to have with yourself and your family: Are you merely dating real estate, or are you committed to building a dynasty?

It's a hard truth that many ignore. Typically, generational wealth follows this familiar story:

- **First Generation:** Works tirelessly to build wealth and lay the foundation.

- **Second Generation:** Inherits the wealth but often lacks the knowledge or skills to manage it.

- **Third Generation:** Squanders it, losing everything because they were never taught how to sustain it.

This cycle repeats when the vital lessons aren't passed down. Just as you wouldn't start a family without preparing to guide and nurture your children, you shouldn't build wealth without a plan to pass it on effectively.

Turning Real Estate Into a Legacy

Building a legacy is more than handing over property deeds. It's about passing down the principles, strategies, and mindset that made your success possible. What you've started is more than a financial transaction; it's a blueprint for your family's future. To ensure sustainable investments, you must involve your heirs, teaching them not just what you've built but how and why you built it.

Start by including them in your decision-making. Show them how to evaluate a property's potential, manage investments responsibly, and identify opportunities for growth. Explain the reasoning behind your strategies—why certain investments were made, how risks were mitigated, and how decisions align with long-term goals.

This isn't just education; it's empowerment. By giving the next generation the tools to make informed decisions, you're equipping them to carry forward your legacy with confidence and clarity.

Planning for the Future

Building a legacy isn't a one-time effort. It's an ongoing commitment to creating systems and structures that preserve and grow your wealth. This means developing clear succession plans, establishing governance structures for family wealth, and implementing strategies for wealth preservation.

It also means preparing for the unexpected. Life is unpredictable, and without a plan in place, even the most carefully built wealth can quickly unravel. By creating clear guidelines for how assets will be managed and passed down, you ensure that your legacy remains intact, even in challenging times.

The Real Happy Ending

Your legacy is not just about the assets you leave behind—it's about the lives you impact, the opportunities you create, and the example you set for those who follow. By planning thoughtfully and involving your family in the process, you ensure that your story continues to inspire and uplift long after you're gone. So ask yourself: Are you building something that will stand the test of time? Or are you simply enjoying the moment?

Your real estate journey is only the beginning. The choices you make now will shape the future for generations to come. Make them count.

CHAPTER 11

Discover Your Co-Buying Solution with Pairgap

"The future of homeownership is shared—and it starts now."
— Nikki Merkerson"

As we close this journey, you've gained the insights, tools, and strategies to navigate the world of co-buying. But knowledge is only the first step. The next is action—and that's where **Pairgap** comes in.

Pairgap simplifies the co-buying process, helping you connect with the right partner, protect your investment, and navigate the real estate ecosystem with confidence. Whether you're co-buying with a friend, family member, or a like-minded individual, Pairgap ensures you're supported every step of the way.

Your Path to Co-Buying with Pairgap

1. Find the Perfect Partner:

Co-buying starts with compatibility. Pairgap helps you vet potential partners with self-assessments and compatibility tools to align goals, values, and financial expectations. If you're unsure about a partner, our detailed vetting process ensures you're teaming up with someone serious and reliable.

2. Protect Your Partnership:

Strong agreements are the foundation of successful co-buying. With our Real Estate Prenup Builder, you can create customized agreements that define contributions, responsibilities, and exit strategies. Pairgap ensures your investment is protected and your expectations are clear.

3. Navigate with Ease:

The real estate world is complex, but it doesn't have to be overwhelming. Pairgap connects you with a trusted network of lenders, agents, attorneys, and other professionals, streamlining the process from pre-approval to closing.

Why Pairgap?

Co-buying doesn't have to feel intimidating or risky. Pairgap removes the guesswork by offering tools and resources tailored to first-time buyers and experienced investors alike. We empower you to make informed decisions, minimize risks, and achieve homeownership on your terms.

Your Next Step

Your co-buying journey doesn't end here—it begins with Pairgap. The tools and concepts you've learned throughout this book can now be put into action with a platform designed to turn your goals into reality.

Ready to take the next step? Visit **Pairgap.com** to start your journey. Whether you're ready to find a partner, create a prenup, or access the best professionals in the real estate market, Pairgap is here to support you every step of the way.

Your dream home is closer than you think. Let Pairgap help you get there.

www.ingramcontent.com/pod-product-compliance
Lightning Source LLC
Chambersburg PA
CBHW010937120626
46554CB00007B/2502